Survival Guide to Living Successfully
The Wacky World

Jacqueline McDonnell, PhD

Yellow Magnolia Press

Yellow Magnolia Press
11 Ancrum Bank, Eskbank, Dalkeith, Midlothian, EH22 3AY

www.yellowmagnoliapress.co.uk

Copyright © Jacqueline McDonnell PhD, 2010
Jacqueline McDonnell has asserted her right under the Copyright, Designs and Patents Act 1988 to be identified as the author of this work.

Photographs of Jacqueline McDonnell on the front cover and with Ricardo Oria Phamie Gow, Henny Dundas and Cheryl Brown courtesy and copyright © Paul Krogh; and of Mr Wu and Suki, in the centre spread, courtesy and copyright © Rob Rogers.
"Mute Swan Pair" woodcarving on driftwood by © Michael Lythgoe, 2010.
Photograph of James Herbert by Julie Dennison © James Herbert.
All other photographs and illustrations © Jacqueline McDonnell.

A CIP catalogue record for this book
is available from the British Library.

ISBN 978-0-9566804-0-2

This book is sold subject to the condition that it shall not, by way of trade or otherwise, be lent, resold, hired out, or otherwise circulated without the publisher's prior consent in any form of binding or cover other than that in which it is published and without a similar condition, including this condition, being imposed on the subsequent purchaser.

Published by the Yellow Magnolia Press 2010
Printed by Minuteman Press, Broomhouse Road, Edinburgh.

Dennis Mary Diarmuid McDonnell

18 May 1932 to 16 April 2002

*Serenely in his sleep,
Dennis the light and love of Jacqueline's life.
Courageous, generous, compassionate, kind,
and with an inimitable
and wicked sense of Irish wit.
Loved by all his family and friends
whose lives have been enriched by his presence;
he made us laugh!
He said: "I am only really happy when I'm with you,"
and his happiness
will rest within my heart forever.*

For Charlie

"One loyal friend is worth ten thousand relatives."
Euripides

and for all of my good friends
who have helped me through
such difficult times.

And with thanks
to
Dorothy Baird, Mark Buckland, Laura Schuster
and Elke Williams
for their support.

Author's Note: A widow, as far as this book is concerned,
is classed as the current spouse, cohabitee or civil partner
of the person who has died.

Friends have given permission for their names to be used.
The accounts in 'The Dating Game' are fictional, loosely inspired by experience.

Contents

- Introduction — page 2
- My Story — page 4
- Memories — page 6
- Who are Your Friends? — page 11
- Old Friends and New Friends — page 12
- Mussels and Buses — page 14
- Moving — page 15

- Get Yourself a Bolt-hole — page 16
- Working Girl — page 17
- Handling Loneliness — page 18
- The Learning Curve — page 22
- Mr Wu and Suki — page 24
- The Dating Game — page 26
- New Adventures — page 32
- Counselling — page 34

- Christmas Fireworks — page 36
- Poetry — page 38
- Take a Look at Yourself — page 47
- Some Quotations — page 49
- Ten Tips for Happier Days — page 50
- Peace in Your Heart — page 51
- People to Contact — page 52

Introduction

I never understood what it meant to be a widow and unless it has happened to you, you cannot understand. I remember when my father died that I had my mother to stay for a few weeks. She hardly left my side and finally one day I took her home because I had the feeling that she needed to get on with her life to start living without my father. Only now do I appreciate how desperately lonely she must have been. She had a few friends and they were helpful for the first months, but then they just faded away and apart from Dennis and myself there was hardly anyone.

As a widow you are an outcast. Not only do you lose the one person in life who was your husband, best friend and soul mate, you also lose your status, certain friends and sometimes your home and certainly your lifestyle. So how can one handle all the situations that arise, the well-meaning but thoughtless remarks, the friends who no longer invite you, the holiday for one, dining alone and all the other challenging moments that come along.

I have, as the song goes, "Survived" and I have only done so by working hard at it. I have called this book "The Wacky World of Widowhood" because is a wacky world; in the dictionary you will find that wacky means eccentric, erratic or unpredictable and the word comes from WHACK, hence a whacky, a person who behaves as if he had been wacked on the head. That is exactly how I feel, as though one day somebody hit me with a sledgehammer. I lost consciousness and when I came to the world had changed and would never ever be the same again; it was full of new, unpredictable situations that I had to come to terms with and often the only thing to do was to see the amusing side of life.

I have two ways of defining the word "widow":

You can be:
Women
In
Despair
Outcast
Women

or:
Women
In
Demand
Outstanding
Women

This book is about moving on from the first definition to the second one. It is about surviving in a new and unpredictable world. I hope it helps.

Jacqueline McDonnell

My Story

This picture, taken by Dennis, sums up happy holidays in Italy in the days when we were both well. We married in 1972 and seven years later I was diagnosed with multiple sclerosis and we lost twins. Having had a career in advertising, I had returned to university late in life and in my final two years took my exams in bed and had to dictate them. I went on to complete a PhD at the University of Edinburgh and then had two books published on Evelyn Waugh. Dennis, in the meantime, developed diabetes, which was manageable for many years. He worked in advertising as a Creative Director and then became Chairman of the company in Scotland before finally going freelance and setting up his own consultancy. In 1992 problems set in and he suffered from heart failure and strokes. Our roles changed; he still looked after me, but I became his main carer and fought a battle to keep him alive for the next ten years. In between I did voluntary work as a children's panel member and then started a children's charity. In 1997 Dennis had a leg amputated. In 1999 I nursed my mother who died of cancer and, shortly after her funeral, I was diagnosed with breast cancer; operations, chemotherapy and radiotherapy followed. Then Dennis's daughter landed up on life support after a hernia operation. In January 2002 Dennis had heart failure again. He recovered only to have his other leg amputated. He contracted MRSA. On April 15, I told him that my cancer review was okay. He died the next morning; his consultants said that he had only waited as long as he had to make sure that I was all right.

His courage was immense. He was everything to me and he is missed.

Your stories will be different to mine: you may be young, middle-aged or elderly, with or without children and grandchildren, and your husband may have died in a war, had a tragic accident, a terminal illness or, like mine, died after many years of ill health.

All of us suffer from grief at losing our partner. All of us have to handle the immediate problems of dealing with the funeral, putting on a brave face for family and friends and, when it is over, facing the fact that life will never be the same again.

Most of us will, unfortunately, have a struggle with money, depending on age and circumstances. Even if we have a pension from our partner's occupation, it will generally only be half of what we were used to living on and the household bills will not be a lot different. If you live by yourself, as I do, you will receive the 25% discount on your council tax, as a single person, but you won't receive that if you still have children living with you, or have anyone else in the house. Single living is expensive too; half of a previous salary doesn't allow for luxuries and when the time comes that you want to get out and about more, it can be hard to make ends meet. There is no doubt that one's lifestyle changes and new ways of living have to be found.

Some of you will be well provided for; others will not be. Some of you will already be working, others of you will need to work to make ends meet. As a widow, widower or civil partner, you may be able to claim bereavement allowance or widowed parents' allowance; please see the details on the last page under "People to Contact."

How do we all handle our grief? The answer is differently. I read about one widow who had a life-size cardboard model of her husband made and took it to an event; you could say that was a "wacky" idea and it's not something I would have done myself, but she believed that it helped her and her children.

Widows of Armed Forces' personnel, heroes who are killed on active service, are now awarded, as the next of kin, the Elizabeth Cross as a mark of the recognition of their loss. Many such widows take up charity work for the forces, which gives them a purpose in life.

Many of us will also think of our husbands or partners as different kinds of "heroes" in the way that they lived their lives and looked after us and our families; and many of them will also have been heroic in the way that they faced their death. We all need a purpose in life and living in a way that would make your husband as proud of you as you were of him is a good way to begin.

Memories

When Dennis died, a couple of months after his second amputation, I could only remember him sitting in bed with no legs, covered with sores and ravaged with pain. It took a long while for me to remember him as the whole man that he had been. For that reason I am going to share three memories here, the first is a memory of a time in hospital shortly before Dennis died, the second is a memory written by my Matron of Honour for our twenty-fifth wedding anniversary, and the third is about a little box.

Mr Frankelfurter

I finally saw Dennis coming on the trolley and then twenty minutes later I was allowed to go in. He appeared fine, smiling that gentle smile, touched my face, my hair, but my heart lurched as I comprehended fully for the first time that he had no legs. This was my man of strength, the man who loved me so deeply, and he was no longer whole. One leg had been bad enough; two was unbearable, and yet he wasn't any different. No legs, but the essential personality was still intact. Not having legs could not destroy that or could it, I wondered? Was his spirit, his fighting spirit still as strong?

He was still suffering from the drugs that they had given him. He thought for some reason that they had taken his leg off to the hip and I had to pull the sheets back and lift him up so that he see that he still had a thigh. He also thought that he had no fingers and kept holding his hands up in front of him. He said that someone in Germany, a Mr Frankelfurter, had taken them. His hands were bandaged to keep the intravenous needle in place as he had a habit of pulling needles out because they hurt and because he associated the line with diamorphine and pain and terror. There was also a blood pressure monitor on his finger, which was emitting an eerie red glow over his hand. He was very

Memories

upset and I told the nurse that she would have to take the monitor and the bandages off so that he could see that he did have fingers. It was heartbreaking. He'd come out of the operation believing that he had no leg left at all and no fingers.

She took the bandages off and I held his hands and counted his fingers with him. He watched, but repeated that he hadn't any fingers, they belonged to Mr Frankelfurter. I said no, they were McDonnell fingers and began counting again: " McDonnell 1, 2,3,4,5 …"

"No," he said, "no fingers, Frankelfurter took them." I began to panic and found myself taking his hand and saying:

"One little piggy went to market,
two little piggies stayed at home,
three little piggies had roast beef,
four little piggies had none and
five little piggies went 'wee wee wee' all the way home."

Dennis looked at me with concern.
"No piggies here," he said. "Have you gone mad?"

Memories

Thoughts from Jill Eakins, Matron of Honour:

"The first time I met Jackie and Dennis they were walking towards me across a piazza in Rome in the bright sunlight. It was back in the days when we were all in the advertising business and earning our living by creating gemlike pieces of prose in praise of frozen fish, soft shampoo and sage and onion stuffing. Jackie and I were copywriters, and Dennis one of those rare and temperamental geniuses known as a Creative Director. No wonder she fell for him. I remember thinking in that piazza in Rome, 'That blonde hair is natural!', which had nothing to do with why he fell for her, of course. I can recall at that first meeting that they were a couple very much in love; and the wonderful thing is that, unlike many others, they have stayed that way.

Immediately we had been introduced, we seemed to gel. This bonding process was probably helped along by the generous quantities of white wine and pasta, which we have continued to consume over the years. It can be no coincidence that the food here today reflects Jackie and Dennis's long love affair with Italy.

I still remember the overall atmosphere of that meeting in Rome. It was, without doubt, one of romance and promise for the future. Even when we returned to the cold light of London, this warm feeling persisted. Jackie and Dennis were 'meant for each other' and they were always the most generous of friends, providing love and support throughout the years. They haven't had the easiest of lives as far as health goes, and yet they have always been fighters and have given each other continuous love and support."

The way we were in 1970.

Memories

The Little Box

The Christmas before Dennis died he gave me, among my gifts, a little box, which had the words on its lid "I'm Only Really Happy When I'm with You." I don't know where he found it, but it reduced me to tears for it was a saying that he had used through all the years that we had known one another.

The day that he was having his second amputation I came home from the hospital for a short while and found the box, which normally sat on the television, in front of the fireplace. I couldn't fathom how it had got there, but I suddenly knew that it was his way of telling me that he was all right. I felt very close to him that day. The box never moved again until after he died and then it happened the night before the funeral and, on a few occasions after that, when I was very upset. The television wasn't switched on so there was no electrical force that was driving its falls to the floor. Perhaps I was doing it telepathically, who knows? Personally I feel that he was there and watching over me.

The last time the box moved my step mother-in-law was with me and I was worrying about whether I should go on a cruise or not. In the middle of the discussion the box flew up in an arc and landed between our two chairs. Eva had always believed my stories about the box, but that time she saw it for herself. I went on the cruise, which was a turning point in my life. Some of you will think this is nonsense, but for others of you who may have experienced some kind of sign or feeling, be happy and take heart in the possibility that you are being watched over.

"I'm Only Really Happy When I'm With You!"

Memories

It is over eight years since my husband died and I still think of him every day, sometimes once a day, often many times a day. For me it is important that he is still brought into conversations, something he said, something he did, because that keeps his spirit alive. When I am writing he is always there. We used to edit each other's work and, when I am struggling for the right word, his voice comes through in my head giving me the answer. I have a built in editor.

    I do remember his birthday, our wedding anniversary, the anniversary of his death, but they are relatively unimportant. What is important is remembering a certain smile, a gesture, the deep laugh, a witty remark, the kindness in his eyes, his generosity of spirit, his courage and determination. You will all have your own memories and you should nurture them. You don't need to dwell on the past; you really need to let go of it, but certain memories are magic moments that can always uplift your heart.

This photograph always makes me laugh. Onwards and upwards!

Who Are Your Friends?

"Misfortune shows those who are not really friends."
Aristotle

Sadly, widowhood teaches you who your friends are. I was fortunate that we had a circle of friends who had supported us through the years of Dennis's ill health and continued to support me after his death; we still spend every New Year's Eve together. However things do change and you find with some friends that you are no longer invited to dinner parties or to the theatre because you are no longer part of a couple; it is hurtful but you have to get used to it. Single people sometimes suffer in this way as well, unless couples are trying to match them with someone.

Thoughtless remarks are common: "We'd invite you to lunch if you had someone to bring!" How are you supposed to conjure up a partner? One widow told me a story where she was invited by the husband of a couple to join them at a dinner dance. She was very vulnerable and it was early on in her widowhood. After sitting by herself for a long time, the husband invited her to dance. On their return to the table his wife hissed: "Can't you get your own man?" If you have ever suffered in this way, or a similar way, smile! It is not you who are the problem; the wife is insecure in her marriage. Widows can be threatening!

Someone I knew berated me because I went away with a man for a weekend six months after I lost my husband. She was angry that I could betray Dennis so quickly. It made me so sad, that she thought that I could, that I didn't tell her that my friend was gay. It was none of her business and she should have known me better, but again it was her problem. She didn't have a man in her life and resented me having another one, as she thought, so quickly.

You can sometimes lose friends because they simply don't know how to handle your grief. "I understand what you must be going through," is a common remark. Another friend had a woman comment when she was mowing her lawn: "I have a husband to do that." Don't fly off the handle, just try to understand that some people don't know what to say and often express themselves badly.

For me certain friends have become my family. Their loyalty is immense and I don't know what I would do without them. I have a friend who is executor of my will and who also has power of attorney for me if it is ever required: I trust him implicitly; and there are other friends who would be there immediately if I needed them, as I would be there for them. Friendship is a two-way street and listening to your friends, rather than giving them your problems all the time, is very important.

Old Friends and New Friends

"It is one of the blessings of old friends that you can afford to be stupid with them."

Ralph Waldo Emerson

How true this is and how many other blessings there are to having friends of long standing. It is so easy to relax and to be yourself with people who have known you for a long time. I have friends I have known for thirty and forty years, who also knew Dennis, and it is wonderful to be able to recall stories about him from the past.

You need to be careful though for it is easy to upset old friends. I remember at the buffet supper at home, the night before Dennis's funeral, that someone commented on the excellent food that was being served and asked who had prepared it. Without thinking, I commented: "There's a new man in my life!" There was, a businessman who dealt with catering, but it came out the wrong way and a few people looked rather shocked. I explained quickly, but when you are tired and grief stricken, it is sometimes easy to get things wrong.

Old friends can be very protective and it can take time for them to realise that you can stand on your own two feet and that you almost need to make mistakes, as you do when you are young, to learn from them. I have a habit of rushing into things and getting fired up with enthusiasm. Sometimes I make the wrong choices, but experience teaches you not to go down that road again.

Recently I had dinner with my old friend Jim, James Herbert, the novelist, who has just received an OBE. He and I worked together 41 years ago and we both worked for my husband. The night was magical for me as he had other old friends from the company there and he told me how much he owed to my husband and how much he thought of him. There were tears that night, but happy ones.

My Matron of Honour, Jill, lives 400 miles away, but we phone each faithfully every week and try to meet once a year. Life would not be the same without her and her husband John or without Bryan, another great friend, who also lost his partner, and with whom I have spent many happy days. Overseas, Lou Magnani, my old boss in New York, still keeps in touch regularly. Seeing people, phoning people, contacting them by email all helps to make life worth living and there is a depth of understanding with old friends. I often call my friend Nancy just at the same time as she is calling me. Old friends are on the same wave length and such friendships are precious for love, trust, loyalty and respect are their essential qualities.

"If a man does not make new acquaintance as he advances through life, he will soon find himself left alone. A man, Sir, should keep his friendship in constant repair."
Samuel Johnson 1709 - 1784

While I was writing this book, I counted up how many new and loyal friends I had made since Dennis died; it amounted to quite a few. It also struck me, after reading the quotation from Samuel Johnson, how many people neglect to make new friends as they grow older. There is almost a fear of being rejected and I have often heard people say:"We have our circle of friends," as though there is no need to have any more or, if they are talking about moving: "It will be hard to make friends."

    Perhaps if Dennis hadn't have died, I would have been the same, but I doubt it as I have always been open to meeting new people. As a widow, however, you are given a new and different life and you will need different people to fulfill your various needs. My husband was my best friend; he was creative, funny and intellectually stimulating; a rare man. I now have new friends who support me, and I them, in different ways. I have friends who are creative; others who debate and argue for hours, some who are highly amusing, some who are particularly kind and caring, some who have fascinating hobbies, some with highly powered jobs and some who are just so relaxing to be with.

    As a newly single person, you need to make friends who are single or who are in a relationship where they have a certain amount of independence. I say this because you need companions, people to share your life with. Your "couple" friends with their various commitments will not always have time for you and it is no good being resentful or envious of their lives; you need a life where they can look at you and sometimes think to themselves: "Gosh, I wish I could do that!"

    New friends will bring you support, warmth, understanding, kindliness and companionship and they may bring new passions and different adventures into your life as you can see in the chapters "New Adventures," and "The Learning Curve."

    New friends are not going to come knocking at your door. You must get out into the world and once you decide to do so, you will be surprised at how many doors open and the delights that are hidden behind them.

" A friend is one to whom one may pour out all the contents of one's heart, chaff and grain together, knowing that the gentlest of hands will take and sift it, keep what is worth keeping and with a breath of kindness blow the rest away."
Arabian Proverb

Mussels and Buses

Written for a special friend:

MUSSELS AND BUSES

I never ate mussels
because I'd been ill.
but you tempted me
to try again.
And now
I love mussels.
There are buses
in Scotland,
which I'd never used,
but we jumped on one.
It got us to Dirleton,
goodness knows why.
But I've been on a bus
now.
Wow -
mussels and buses -
what else will I try?

Moving

This is my beautiful spring garden, ablaze in all its glory, and I nearly left it and my house to move to a flat. I was doing a lot in town, so it seemed sensible to move away, and to start a new life in the city centre. Luckily, I realised in time that my house was my home and I didn't want to move from my community and all the support that I had around me. The flat wouldn't really have been suitable for my dogs either.

Moving is a big step and one that has to be thought about very carefully. I made the decision too soon after Dennis died, but moving for some of you will be the right thing to do. I know widows who have upped sticks and made new and exciting lives for themselves and moving from the known to the unknown can be a powerful and rewarding experience. Again you need to be prepared to work hard at your new life as you will have to make new friends, join new organisations and develop plenty of interests. Don't make the mistake of moving just to be near family; it doesn't always work out and, for whatever reason, they may need to move in the future. Move to somewhere where you are not dependent on someone and where you know that you will be able to look after yourself. Look around you and make sure of what you are doing: downsizing to a smaller place locally may be better than moving many miles away.

I think there may well come a time when I reach a crossroads and need to move, but fate will take a hand and lead me to make the right decision.

Get Yourself a Bolt-Hole

My retreat when I am sad and lonely is to go to the sea. I find peace in the power of the ocean and the changing tides, the calmness one day, the stormy waves the next. I was lucky enough to have a caravan where I could sit and look at the view for hours. For a while I bolted from my house to the beach, would stay for a while and then have to go home again. There is something strange in the first years of widowhood where you are restless and can't settle in one place. I needed space away from people when I couldn't handle life. The caravan has now been sold and I am comfortable at home, but there are still times when I drive out to the ocean with the dogs and take a few hours for myself.

Your bolt-hole may be walking in the country, or driving somewhere. I have a friend who loves a particular view over the Lammermuir hills, another who enjoys sitting by the calmness of a river. The place has to be one where you can get away and be with yourself, a place that will ease your troubled heart and give you some space to heal yourself; it may be a quiet spot in your local park, the garden of a country house, a bluebell wood, a church, anywhere that will help to give you inner peace.

Working Girl

It is important to make a contribution to life and working, whether it is paid or voluntary, will help you to keep your sanity in these, the darkest of days. Having somewhere to go, something to do, provides you with a reason to get up in the morning, to interact with people, to have a purpose in life.

For many years I ran a small charity called "The Friends of Midlothian's Children." Myself and my colleagues, now all good friends, worked on a voluntary basis. We had no paid staff and we were all dedicated to raising funds for respite care for local children in need. We provided four mobile homes at different holiday parks and supplied over 125 family holidays a year. Recently at an awards ceremony, pictured above, we handed everything over to the agencies with whom we worked and they are now successfully running the holidays themselves.

If you have a job, get back to it when you feel able to. Your colleagues will support you and if, after a while, you decide that you need a different environment, you can take your time to look for something else. If you don't work, consider a voluntary position. Whether working in a charity shop, or being an adviser with the Citizen's Advice Bureau, there are plenty of jobs to choose from and your local Volunteer Bureau can help you. Without my voluntary work, I would have been lost. I had people to meet, funds to raise, caravans to buy; goals to achieve. There wasn't time to worry about myself.

In the picture taken by Paul Krogh, a great friend, are Henny Dundas, patron of the charity, Jacqueline, and Cheryl Brown of Midlothian Sure Start receiving an award.

Handling Loneliness

So now you are on your own. You may be fortunate to have children to keep you company and family and friends who support you, but when the children are in bed and the family and friends have gone home, the front door closes and you are left with another evening of loneliness and heartache. Perhaps you have been out for the evening and come in and there is no one to talk to, no one to relay the details of the occasion to, good or bad. I miss talking to Dennis. I miss coming in and saying: "Darling, you won't believe what happened tonight?"

What does "loneliness" mean then? It is a word that refers to a lack of companionship, but it goes deeper than that because it often signifies a feeling of unhappiness, despair, grief, and a lack of fulfillment. "Lonely" is different from "solitary," which is often a choice, rather than a condition which is imposed upon one. Somebody who is solitary by nature often prefers their own company to that of other people.

A girl standing in a theatre foyer by herself can feel lonely in the midst of a crowd, but loneliness can also be a state of mind, a feeling induced by the lack of someone special in one's life, the lack of a close relationship. It can cause sadness, depression, hurt and bewilderment at the state that one finds oneself in.

Your friends and family often don't understand your loneliness. If, like me, you are often out doing things, they exclaim: "But how can you be lonely, you have so many interests, so many friends." If you're a widow with children they think you are fortunate because you still have your children to keep you company, never mind the fact that children don't talk like adults. Also, because it hasn't happened to them they will never understand the despair of going to bed with no partner to cuddle. No one to hold you close in his arms, to love and

Unwanted solitude

cherish you as the most important person in his life and he the most important person in yours.

Some widows, like myself, are completely alone, no parents, no siblings, no children. I have three stepchildren, but only my stepdaughter, whom I love dearly, is close and she lives many miles away, as indeed does my caring step mother-in-law. Geography plays a part in all of our lives these days.

So how are lonely widows different to other lonely people? They are not. Many widows often put themselves in a special category thinking that the loss of their partner is a more extreme version of loneliness, but I know people who have never experienced the kind of companionship that I had. You can drown in your sorrow or wake up and live again, be positive and realise that you had a great partner, a great life and that is something that nobody can take away from you! Finding Dennis was the best thing that ever happened to me and recognising how good your life was together, whether it was six months, six years or sixty years is the beginning to healing. The question is never: "Why me?" The question is: "Why not me?"

These days 25% or more of the people around you probably feel the same way. Single, separated, and divorced people can feel isolated and many people also feel alone in a marriage or partnership. Loneliness in a relationship is often not the physical fact of someone not being there, but the fact of two people no longer having anything in common with one another. Millions of people in the world live by themselves these days and we all need to find answers to handling our loneliness. I am not going to tell you that I have found a miracle cure. I haven't, but over the years I have established a number of ways to help with the problem.

Handling Loneliness

Help someone else! To be needed is a large answer to loneliness. Judy Garland said: "Loneliness and the feeling of being unwanted is the most terrible poverty," but there are plenty of people who could do with your help and one of the answers is to volunteer, as giving of yourself enables others to give back to you.

Be pro-active, get out and engage with people! Speak to people on the telephone, talk to people in shops. Driving one day and feeling blue, I remember listening to a radio programme on shyness and meeting new people. The advice was to talk to three strangers every day. I started immediately. In an Oxfam shop in Edinburgh there was a large chap in a black cloak and a black fedora with long grey hair and a beard. I tapped him on the shoulder and said that he looked rather like a friend of mine, but my friend didn't have the amazing cloak and hat, where had he got them? He was rather surprised, but delighted to talk. He was a poet from Cork in the west of Ireland and was going to a conference on the "Da Vinci Code," which was being held not far from where I lived. We chatted for ages and he suggested that I should join the conference. I didn't do so, but that first conversation broke the ice and I have been talking to people ever since.

Express your feelings! Too many of us bottle up our feelings when a loved one dies. If you can express your grief, your loss and loneliness, it will bring your feelings to the surface and in the long run make them easier to handle. Don't be afraid to say to family or friends that you need to meet, to go out, or just to have a chat. Remember that many people don't know how to help you and are afraid of doing the wrong thing. If you can be honest with yourself and with others, life will be easier for everyone.

Change yourself! We were known as Dennis and Jackie. I am still Jackie to my old friends, but I decided to return to my preferred name of "Jacqueline" for my voluntary work and for new friends. It was easier to be identified as the new single Jacqueline than as part of a couple. A makeover can help. My husband had always liked me with long hair, but for a while I cut it short. I felt different and freer. A friend of mine was overweight when she was widowed and decided to take herself in hand. She lost three stone and looked ten years younger. It improved her well being and gave her a new outlook on life. She has since met a new partner and feels that it was partly because of her new found confidence. It is hard to get out and meet people and sometimes creating a "new you" can help.

Stay connected! When you are alone, it is easy to feel isolated and there are things you can do to make life better. It is important to feel in touch with the world. Try listening to the radio; it is different to television because you need to use your imagination more. Music is often helpful because it provides an avenue for you to communicate with a deeper part of yourself. You can find solace and hope in your favourite pieces. If you have a dog, take it out and talk to other dog owners. If you have a computer, use the internet, tap into a chat line, or trace your family tree, but don't get isolated with virtual friends! You need real people! If you find yourself unbearably miserable, go to a film or a gallery, have people around you, but lose yourself in another world.

Take stock of your life! You may be in good health, be financially secure, have a pleasant home, a helpful family, plenty of friends. Even if you only have one or two of these things, you are fortunate. It doesn't make loneliness easier necessarily, but it means that there are other people out there who have more problems than you do. Remember, we come into the world alone and we go out alone. What we make of the world while we are here is up to us!

The Learning Curve

I have always believed in expanding my horizons, but being widowed is the biggest learning curve there is. You have to learn how to live alone, to make decisions for yourself, to resolve problems, to manage your financial affairs, to understand the reactions of your friends, to prepare meals for one, and to try to be constantly cheerful and not a miserable cow: it's a lot to ask.

Amongst all this there has to be some fun and that's where the real learning challenge comes in, for by developing new skills you will meet many more people. The more you learn, the more potential you have to unlock your dreams and to enjoy a brighter future. In the eight years since my husband's death I have tried numerous classes and courses. I studied the harp and the piano. I joined a choir. I have experimented with yoga, pilates, tai chi, ballet and tango. I now have a smattering of Spanish and Italian. I have enjoyed courses in drawing and painting. I attend all kinds of lectures. I belong to a book group, a creative support group and a poetry group. I joined a supper club, a nightclub, and took out memberships to galleries. I have learnt how to meditate. I tried to learn bridge, but failed dismally. I went on cookery courses. Gliding for the disabled called for a day, but never again; I was absolutely terrified. I studied screenwriting and learnt about publishing.

This year I am trying the Alexander Technique and I am trying to track down a laughing class, for laughing raises serotonin levels and reduces stress. People who can laugh at life are happy and seem to have far less risk of stress-associated problems. Exercise can also help as it releases endorphins that help to lift our mood. Walking, swimming and going to the gym can all be helpful and learning an exciting new sport such as skiing, flying, riding or surfing, for example, can be a wonderful new challenge.

I am grateful as well to the many young people who have made my life so much more bearable over the last few years; many of them have become

There's So Much Out There!

close friends, and we learn from one another. Phamie Gow, pictured below, taught me the harp. I had always loved the instrument and after attending a number of concerts at a Harp Festival in Edinburgh, I decided to go ahead and try. Phamie was patient and we became great friends. I don't play now, but I follow her career with love and interest. She benefits from my experience of the world and I benefit from her passion for her music and her enthusiasm for life.

Getting out and learning something new both stimulates you and gives you the chance to meet new people. It would be very strange if, in a class or group full of people interested in the same subject, you didn't connect with a like-minded person. You may not make great friends immediately, but you will make acquaintances and some of these relationships will develop; on top of that you will enhance your learning curve and have fun!

Photograph of Phamie, by Paul.

Mr Wu and Suki

Mr Wu, on the left, is twelve years old and was bought after my husband had had his first leg amputated. Our huge bearded collie had cancer whilst Dennis was ill and had to be put to sleep, as though life wasn't difficult enough at the time. Friends said it was

Mr Wu and Suki by Rob Rogers

stupid to get another dog, that Dennis wouldn't manage and would fall over it. My husband thought that was silly, his logic being that a puppy would as easily skirt around one leg and a frame, or crutches, as it would two legs. He was right and Mr Wu took pride of place in the house. Often when I came in, I would find the two of them, Wu on Dennis's lap, fast asleep in the conservatory. How did Mr Wu get his name? It was Lady Diana Cooper's nickname for Evelyn Waugh, which she had told me about during an interview. Mr Wu was Chinese and our little dog was a Tibetan Lhasa Apso; somehow the name just fitted. The Christmas before Dennis died, he asked me what I wanted for a present and I said another Lhasa Apso. We both knew in our hearts that he may not have a lot longer and he agreed to my wish, believing that another little dog would occupy me and be good company. Suki, on the right, arrived in time for

Saving My Life!

Christmas and was a monster, biting Wu, tearing the house up and generally behaving badly, although her melting eyes have always made her look as though she couldn't possibly do anything wrong, absolutely innocent.

After Dennis died the two of them saved my sanity. I couldn't lie in my bed in the morning wallowing in grief, they wanted up and to be fed, watered and played with. When I came in with a heavy heart they were there bouncing around the place, overjoyed to see me. They made life worthwhile and they understood. For months after Dennis died Mr Wu would sit at the bottom of the stairs crying and I believe that there were times that Dennis was there in his study and the dog knew. Mr Wu certainly knew when Dennis was dying and the night before he went to hospital he wouldn't leave his side. Nowadays they won't leave me. Whichever room I am in they are there too and they travel with me. They protect me as well and certainly let me know if they don't approve of someone.

A young widow friend of mine, I will call her Caroline, was distraught when her husband died and a friend suggested a little rescue dog, a Yorkshire terrier. My friend wasn't sure, but when she saw Betsy she recognised the pain in the little dog's eyes as her own pain and took the poor little creature home. Betsy was her saving grace and she later got another Yorkie to keep Betsy company while she was at work. My friend also thought that her dogs enabled her to move on with life: "Betsy was a wee scrap, emaciated, weak, we needed each other. Betsy flourished, ate gourmet food and loved going on walks. People talked to us. Having the dogs helped me to lead a more normal life." Caroline was fortunate that she met a new partner and sadly Betsy died shortly before she moved in with him. Her partner used to joke: "I have two Yorkies every day," meaning Yorkie bars of course, but Caroline had wondered how he would get on with two dogs. When Betsy was dying, Caroline strongly felt that the dog was ready to go: "It's time for me to go mum, my job has been done. I looked after you while you were alone."

I know widows who have cats and a widow who has a canary, as she is not allowed a dog or a cat in the flat where she lives. It doesn't matter what kind of pet you have, a living being in the house helps; it is something for you to care for and who, in turn, cares about you.

There was a George Formby song: "Oh Mr Wu what shall I do, I'm hanging out those Chinese Laundry Blues." My Mr Wu has definitely, as has Suki, helped me to deal with my blues, maybe a pet can help you with yours.

The Dating Game

Dating may well seem utterly unthinkable in your darkest hours but, young or old, many of you will decide, at some point, that you don't want to be alone forever and may hope to find love and a new partner.

Some widows get involved very quickly with someone new and it can cause problems both for the widow, who may not really be ready for the relationship, and for her family and friends who could resent the newcomer; such a situation needs to be handled with kid gloves because at these early stages you are extremely vulnerable and it is really easy to make the wrong decision. To be wanted again by someone is lovely, but is that all it is about? With death comes the need to reassert life and some of us need to establish who we are and why we are here; it's called life force and is an entirely natural reaction.

So how do you start meeting men again? There are a large number of dating sites on the internet and there are plenty of introduction agencies, ranging from those who specialise in personal introductions to agencies who run events from dinner dances to hill walking weekends. Three years after Dennis died I tried a supper club, the internet, and an introduction agency; none of them worked because I simply wasn't ready to date again and I also felt very strongly that if someone were meant to come into my life, it would happen naturally. This does not mean that it has to be the same for you, many people form good relationships with friends they have met on the web; and maybe "friends" is the telling word. The WAY (Widowed and Young) Foundation is a good support group where you can meet other widows and widowers online and it also holds events. Such a group helps you to make friends with people in a similar situation who understand your feelings. You will find WAY'S contact details at the back of his book.

I had some amusing experiences, which you can read about here, but all the people who have come into my life since Dennis died have been through my voluntary work, classes of different kinds, travel, and contacts through friends. I have met one or two men whom I enjoyed spending time with, but I would not want to spend my life with them. It is not a matter of comparing people to Dennis for that is something one must never do: a new relationship has to be *new* and *different* from what went before; comparisons will only cause heartache. The other really important thing to remember is that if you do meet someone else, you shouldn't feel guilty about betraying the memory of your loved one. You will never forget him and he would want you to have another chance of happiness.

A Whole New World!

The Intruder

A black day, I am depressed and I hurt. There is a pain in my chest, a heavy lump, which will not go away and all because I met a man. I tried to start dating again.

He came to tea. At 67 he was reasonably attractive. He had a strong face and good eyes and teeth. He was too slight for my liking, but what was the real problem?

He didn't like the dogs.

He pushed them aside with a contemptuous gesture. He said his ex-wife had dogs who were horribly spoilt and that he was a disciplinarian: "Dogs weren't humans, they had to be kept in their place." The dogs understood. They followed us into the conservatory and jumped up on the sofa, much to his disgust, and then they sat there and glowered. Four large expressive brown eyes fixed themselves on the intruder.

He didn't belong. He sat in the chair that my husband used to sit in, the chair that now all my good male friends choose to sit in, and he talked. How he talked. He was a fitness fanatic and believed that his good health was all due to hard work. Nine fruit and vegetables a day, but he didn't cook, chops were his limit. He came from a Baptist family and was considered to be the black sheep. He may have been wild in his time, but now he was yawning dull.

He wore brown brogues and short beige socks.

Mr. Wu barked.

"Why is he doing that?"

"He wants you to go!" I said.

The Dating Game

Answer-phone

"Shit ...

Jacqueline ...

Hi - it's Freddie ...

I've completely forgotten that I had to ring you at ten to one.

I've just answered my mobile and using it made me realise I should have called you...

You're on the phone so I presume you're still alive.

Anyway you better get in touch ... soon...cheers..."

This is just to remind you that it is very important to leave details of where you are meeting your contact with a member of your family or a trusted friend. If you decide to go anywhere else, be sure to phone and let them know that there is a change of plan. Make sure you meet in a busy place and preferably just for a drink or coffee on the first occasion, which gives you a chance to get out of the situation if there is no connection, or if you feel uncomfortable.

Unkind Regards

Do I laugh, or do I cry? Laughter is the only way, so here I am nearly choking on it and the tears are running down my face, so the crying is taking place too.

I have been with an introduction agency for five months. I went a few years after my husband died to see if it was possible to form a friendship with another man. After 30 years of a happy marriage, this was a difficult thing to do and had taken a certain amount of courage.

I met the woman who ran the business. She was short, stout, cropped black hair, open pores and dressed in maroon polyester. "Was I too old at sixty-five"? I asked. No, there were fewer men, but she could think of plenty of professional ones on her books who would be interested in a charming, sophisticated woman like myself. She said I was attractive with a good personality and sense of humour and she would be in touch. It wasn't cheap, £300 down and £30 a month standing order. I pointed out that I didn't want a sports fanatic as I had some health problems and could not join in sporting activities. I also specified tall men, professional men, and men who were widowed, divorced or single, but not separated. At my age I did not want to get involved with any more baggage than necessary.

The first man was about my height, ran marathons, sailed, played golf and went hill-walking, a veritable sports enthusiast.

The next man was separated and lived a hundred miles away. I said no. She didn't take too kindly to this saying that she was sure that there would be a divorce soon.

The third man didn't want to see me, fair enough.

The Dating Game

The fourth man, by now it was four months in to this non-dating arena, was in Ceylon and not expected back for a while. I pointed out that this was hardly satisfactory. She promised many more men in the New Year.

Six weeks later a picture came through of the fifth man, an Irishman living in Dublin. He was a lot shorter than myself. I telephoned and said that he didn't meet any of the requirements. She said he was really pleasant. Had she met him? No, he was still in Ireland. One of her selling points was that everyone had to be interviewed by her personally before they could join.

I had had enough. My bank balance was lighter by £450. I cancelled the standing order and emailed her and asked for a refund.

She said there would be no refund and what did I expect? I was in my sixties after all and no oil painting!

Clearly I need a mask!
Painting: *"Red Mask"* by J.McDonnell

There are Success Stories!

Yes, you can fall in love again, or learn to love someone else. A friend of mine joined an introduction agency and after meeting a few men, whom she had nothing in common with, suddenly met the right person. She is now living with him and the relationship is a success.

Someone else I know joined their local walking club, similar to the Ramblers' Club, and met a widower who became a great companion. They do not live together, but they enjoy having dinner and going to the theatre, as well as regularly joining their other friends on their Saturday walks. Who knows what the future holds?

I also heard the story of a young widow who joined her local gym to get herself fit. She couldn't believe that at her hottest and sweatiest, a man appeared to be interested in her. After chatting to her for a few times, he finally asked her out for a drink and after a few months they moved in together.

I said previously that you need to careful in the early and vulnerable days and I also said that sometimes support groups can help. I know of two cases where couples met because they were going to a cancer hospice every day to be with their dying partners. After their respective partners died, they joined the support group at the Marie Curie and consoled each other. They were vulnerable, but they understood each other's stories and in both cases they ended up by getting married.

Fate will take a hand in all of this and if you are meant to meet someone, you will do so. Remember though that there are always paths to choose, but you need to get out of the house to walk them!

New Adventures

Long before my husband died we talked about the fact that I had always wanted an MGB and he told me that he would try to get me one in the future. After he had gone, and as my mother had left me some money, I decided to buy one. Fate took a hand. After contacting many dealers, I went to see a car and couldn't believe that its license plate began with 'MDC.' Somebody joked that it stood for Midlothian District Council, but it was near enough to McDonnell for me. I think Dennis had a hand in it. I had a great time with the car, driving round the hills in the evenings and going for rides to the coast. Young men tried to overtake me on the motorway, but didn't realise that the car had a three and a half litre, V8 engine. Their faces were a picture when I put my foot down! I should have written a book called "The Adventures of an MGB and Two Llasa Apsos" as the dogs absolutely loved riding on the back seat. The car had had to be changed to an automatic because of my multiple sclerosis and, when it was time to sell it, I was quite worried as I thought it might have to be converted back again. Luckily somebody in the MG club needed one and it went to a good home! It also inspired a very short poem called "The End of the Affair":

You're not the man for me, so I've bought an MGB!

New adventures are so important. I tried to learn tango without a great deal of success; shaky legs don't help! I did however became great friends with Ricardo, the young Argentinian who ran the class, who was 23 at the time. He invited me to go to Buenos Aires to meet his family. He wanted me to understand where he had been brought up. My first reaction was that I couldn't

Small and Large!

possibly do that, but I quickly realised that it was a huge honour that he was bestowing on me and I decided to bite the bullet and go! I had a magical time with Ricardo and his girlfriend Jenny. I was then a witness at their marriage in Edinburgh and they now have a wonderful baby boy. I feel so fortunate to have them as friends.

It is clear to me that you can do anything you want to do; you just have to have the gumption! Don't say: " I couldn't do that," just say: "Why couldn't I do that"? You turn things on their head and suddenly there are a hundred solutions.

In these last years I have been to France, Spain, New York, Florida and New Zealand, as well as going on a Mediterranean cruise and taking many trips around the British Isles. I have flown over the Iguassu Falls and the Bay of Islands, but I haven't yet been to Alaska, swum with dolphins or learnt how to fly and maybe those, for me, are going to be the next adventures!

Attempting the tango with Ricardo at a charity reception! Photograph by Paul!

Counselling

Painting: *"Two of Me"* by J.McDonnell

There may come a time when you need someone professional to talk to. I thought I was fine, working away, convincing myself that everything was all right until seven years after Dennis died, I cracked and cracked seriously. I started having suicidal thoughts and could no longer face the memories of what had happened to him. My doctor thought it was post traumatic stress disorder and recommended some counselling; in the depths of despair, I agreed. The image here, painted by me, shows how I discovered, through my talks with a therapist, that I had become two people; the first an extroverted person and the other one, a suppressed creative person, a shadow of the extrovert, always pushed down and never let out to play. My hard working extroverted self was my way of managing, but the real creative me was crying out to be heard again. After a number of sessions I took note and decided to change my life. It was time to cut back on the work, to start writing again and to have some fun.

When a loved one dies you lose part of yourself and it takes a while to both discover and to create your new self. Dennis had his legs amputated, but

A Time and a Place

when he died I felt that part of me had been severed and it took a long time to put myself back together again.

There is a time and place for counselling and it could range from early on to years later. Only you will know when you feel ready to ask for help. You may want to see a therapist by yourself, or you may want to join a group of other people. There are excellent bereavement services available such as those run by "Cruse" and if your partner died of a specific illness there are groups run by Marie Curie for the relatives of cancer sufferers and groups for Parkinson's and other illnesses. Your doctor can put you in touch with your local services, or you can contact the National Association of Widows, their contact details are given at the back of this book.

Counselling can create a turning point in your life and open you up to a whole new range of experiences. For me, it meant taking off on a cruise and being ready for some "Christmas Fireworks."

Christmas Fireworks

Before I had my counselling, I had already booked a cruise for the Christmas of 2008. Christmas is the loneliest time. You can be surrounded by people, family, friends, but the one person who matters isn't there. Having spent six years making sure that I wouldn't be alone at Christmas, I decided to go to go on a cruise, to do something different. The nearer the time approached the more I dreaded it. I thought it was going to be a disaster, but I was wrong. I was sixty-six young, looking for some fun and I found it. I met a man who turned my life around. No, I didn't have an affair, fall madly in love, or get married. I met someone from the other side of the world who liked me and I liked him.

Memories are made of such occasions as this: like a scene from *The Titanic*, two people high up on the deck of the ship, everyone else below, watching a spectacular firework display, the ship anchored off Madeira. Midnight struck and kisses took place. For the first time in seven years I responded to a man. He woke me up, broke the chains, and I was alive again.

My friend invited me to spend a month with him in New Zealand. Amidst warnings and worries, I went. What at 67 (now) had I to lose. He was a gentleman, courteous, kind, witty and wise. If it didn't work out, I could always go off and explore the country by myself. It took courage and it worked. We became good friends. It was an interlude, a magical time of finding that I was attractive to someone again and of leading that charmed life of being a couple for a month. I met his family and his friends and he whirled me round the country, taking me to wonderful places, treating me to memorable events like flying over the Bay of Islands and all the time being so kind, so generous

and Other Holidays

and so attentive. I came home to my solitary existence, apart from the company of my two little dogs, but life had changed. I have stopped driving myself. I am learning to relax. I am beginning to enjoy my own company. A close friend recently asked me how "Lover Boy" was and I answered "Fine." My New Zealander will always be special for he enriched my life and helped me to move on.

The following Christmas my old and very dear friend, Bryan, came to stay and I threw a party for fifteen close friends on New Year's Eve, something I never would have done previously.

These special holidays are not easy, but Christmas Day is only one day in the year. If you are fortunate enough to have family and children, try to enjoy them and think how much your partner would have loved to have been there. Try not to feel sad, feel happy for those around you and you will begin to feel a spark of happiness in yourself. If you don't have anywhere to go at Christmas, make the most of a relaxing day at home with good food, a good book and a good film. If you can't bear to be alone, either join a singles Christmas break or go out and help someone else. "Crisis at Christmas" and other voluntary organisations are always looking for people to help.

Going on holiday is also difficult and I have mixed feelings about going with a friend. Sharing a room doesn't always work out and sometimes you want to explore on your own. Being alone often has its advantages as there is no one to tie you down and you meet many more people. Going by yourself or with a group forces you to talk to new people and that has to be good. There are plenty of holidays for single people these days and you have the world to choose from. I believe that it is also sensible to go to new places; returning to romantic spots that you have been to in the past will not help your recovery. The joy of going somewhere new means new experiences and new experiences are the life blood of living.

Poetry

Dennis

His face comes in the night.
He steals between the sheets
and lies with me.
His spirit warms the bedclothes
his courage heats my blood
and strengthens me.
Once he was gaunt, grey
full of pain.
Now he is free.

Green Pastures

I long to see my husband again:
wild, wild Irishman
full of laughter and Celtic sorrow.

I long to see his legs
striding out in green pastures,
not severed at the thighs
thrown in a bin.

I long to see rivers of healing,
white swans gliding faithfully,
not black adders
eating at his heart and mind.

I long to see my husband again,
him,
only him,
whole in my mind.

"Mute Swan Pair" Woodcarving on driftwood by Micheal Lythgoe, 2010

Summer Ice

Long summer days tear at my soul
for loneliness is summer ice,
cracking my heart
with its freezing solitude
watching couples
enjoying sun-kissed life.

When heat beats my body
to a wrung out lemon
I adjourn to the safeness of a cool fanned room
to lie and dream
of what summer could be like.

The Merry Widow

She talks, she smiles, she laughs a lot,
the centre of a crowd.
She's hardly pining people think
as she downs another drink.
But when you see her unawares,
you'll see her face forlorn.
For in repose the truth is there:
every day is hard to bear.

Her husband was her joy, her life.
She was his beloved wife.
Now she's lonely, lost and sad,
sometimes feels a little mad.
Then someone breaks her reverie,
the smile appears, the show goes on -
the widow sings her merry song
and those who know her cry along.

Widow's Weeds

The black I wore was playful, nonchalant,
designer gear in shades of black:
Ebony, Charcoal, Raven, Jet
in silks and satins, cashmere and cotton.
Strange partners then,
these garments hanging side by side
with the darker plainer clothes,
found in wardrobes
when death arrives.

Swirling skirts that skimmed the floor,
others grazing soft tanned thighs.
Long lean jeans,
plunging shirts,
black was not a focus, a necessity -
it was a statement of desire,
of design, of individuality.
A widow's black is dull,
buttoned up;
a widow's black
is death in perpetuity.
It's not my style.

The people-crows wait,
solemn faces, sighs and tears.
High black heels descend.
A Jackie Kennedy dress and coat,
shocking pink buttons,
shocking pink pillbox hat.
Smoky grey eyes peering from beneath
a frail lace curtain,
a bold red mouth,
bright red nails under black lace mittens.
As the whispers start to grow,
I hear my husband in my heart –
that's my girl!

The Widow Lane

Some men put me in the slow lane.
They take their time,
informing friends
that patience pays off,
that a widow will succumb,
the apple will fall off the tree.

Others take the middle lane.
They become my friend,
but their true desires
show themselves in due course.
And when I say
" slow down,"
they seem surprised,
the friendship comes to a crossroads,
and no one knows which road to take.

Some men take the fast lane.
They press their bodies close to mine,
sure that I am hot for love.
And when I turn away,
they become defensive,
saying I gave them
The green light to go ahead.

Put on the brakes, chaps!
Halt, right there.
My life is in the widow lane.
I'm not to be taken slowly,
at an average speed,
or at a hundred miles an hour.
I am at a junction in my life.
I am travelling in the widow lane
and only I will know
when I reach my destination.
The road is mine.

Beach road in New Zealand

Wild Side

Painting:
"Blue Mask" by J. McDonnell

The blue widow woman
has a wild, wild side.

In darkest clothes,
she smoulders deep inside.

Cool and calm and sensible,
that's what you see,

but the widow woman isn't me.

I buried my loving husband
and society buried me.

Now the wild woman is stirring,
the wild woman within me.

Take a Look at Yourself

In many companies people use a SWOT analysis to determine the strengths and weaknesses of the business, the opportunities that exist and the possible threats. Not so long ago, I decided to do a SWOT analysis for myself. My strengths, weaknesses, opportunities and threats are listed below and I have left space for you, over the page, to fill in your own thoughts. In this analysis, strengths and weaknesses are to be seen as internal factors, part of your own make up, and opportunities and threats are the external factors that may affect your life. After compiling your list, think about the opportunity that you would like to action for yourself and how you could achieve it by building on your strengths and addressing the weaknesses and threats in your life.

STRENGTHS
Creative
Making new contacts
Achieving goals
Just me

WEAKNESSES
Discipline
Patience
Fear of the unknown
Just me

OPPORTUNITIES
New job
New friends
New interests

THREATS
Lack of skills
Finances
Isolation

ACTION PLAN
I had made new friends and had plenty of interests so I decided that my opportunity would be a new job, which would be a publishing business. My strengths of being creative, able to make new contacts and achieving goals would help. A strength and a weakness was that the business would just be me working on my own. Cutting out the middle-men would potentially make me more money, but working by myself would be isolating and there would be no one to bounce ideas off. There was also my fear of the unknown, of how the publishing business worked these days, and the fact of not being as disciplined as I needed to be to meet deadlines. I decided to do a publishing course, which was fun and enlightening. It taught me about self publishing and the new ways of selling books. It also introduced me to people who shared the same enthusiasm and who were happy to share their experiences. Taking a step into the unknown suddenly didn't seem quite so difficult after all. I also began

Take a Look at Yourself

some business courses to develop new skills. The threat of isolation receded as I met more like-minded people. The threat of financial insecurity was harder as how did one finance a new business? I decided to sell some possessions, rather than take out a loan. The business, "The Yellow Magnolia Press," is now up and running and is the challenge for the future. It has given me a new focus.

That's me, how about you? What opportunities are you looking for? New friends? A new relationship? A new hobby? A new job? Fill in the opportunities section first, decide on the area you would like to develop, and then add in the strengths, weaknesses and threats that you think apply. After that fill in the action plan. Remember, once you have set your mind to something, it can be achieved!

STRENGTHS   **WEAKNESSES**

OPPORTUNITIES   **THREATS**

ACTION PLAN

Some Quotations

"When widows exclaim loudly against second marriages, I would always lay a wager that the man, if not the wedding-day, is absolutely fixed on."

Henry Fielding 1707 - 1754

"These widows, Sir, are the most perverse creatures in the world."

Joseph Addison 1672 - 1719

"The rich widow cries with one eye and rejoices with the other."

Miguel de Cervantes 1547 - 1616

"I have been to a funeral; I can't describe to you the howl which the widow set up at proper intervals."

Charles Lamb 1775 - 1834

"Widows, like ripe fruit, drop easily from their perch."

Jean de La Bruyere 1645 - 1696

"Rich widows are the only secondhand goods that sell at first-class prices."

Benjamin Franklin 1706-1790

"Widow. The word consumes itself - "

Sylvia Plath 1932 - 1963

Ten Tips for Happier Days

You can't live life worrying about what will happen in the future. You need to live life for the experience of travelling through it and being open to whatever may come your way. Keep your partner in your heart, but allow yourself to look with clear eyes to the future; a future that is full of potential. Try to:

1. Live each day as it comes.
2. Keep a balance in your life.
3. Put your alone time to good use.
4. Meditate - calmness brings clarity.
5. Go out and meet new people.
6. Laugh.
7. Learn to love your independence.
8. Have adventures.
9. Congratulate yourself on your achievements.
10. Eat a cream bun without worrying about your waistline.

Peace in Your Heart

Life will never be the same again, but it can still be enjoyed and cherished. Your grief will eventually ease, the intensity of it will lessen and you may form a new relationship. Some widows choose to stay alone; others find a new partner. Healing takes time but with the support of others, and with your own determination, you will overcome the pain and start living again.

"Nothing should be prized more highly than the value of each day."

Goethe

May there always be work for your hands to do, may your purse always hold a coin or two. May the sun always shine on your widowpane, may a rainbow be certain to follow each rain. May the hand of a friend always be near you, may God fill your heart with gladness to cheer you.

Irish Blessing

People to Contact

The National Association of Widows
National Office, 48 Queens Road, Coventry, CV1 3EH
Call 024 7663 4848 www.widows.uk.net

The WAY Foundation (Widowed and Young) Suite 35, St Loyes House, 20 St Loyes Street, Bedford MK40 1Z Call 0870 011 3450 www.wayfoundation.org.uk

Care for the Family: Call 029 2081 0800 www.careforthefamily.org.uk

The War Widows' Association of Great Britain
c/o 199 Borough High Street, London SE1 1AA
Call 0845 2412 189 www.warwidowsassociation.org.uk

There is also the **Army Widows' Association** www.armywidows.org.uk , the **RAF Widows' Association** www.rafwidowsassociation.org.uk and the **Royal Navy Royal Marines Widows' Association** www.rnrmwidowsassociation.org

Cruse Bereavement Care Telephone 0844 477 9400
www.crusebereavementcare.org.uk

Bereavement Benefits claim pack, form BB1 can be ordered over the telephone from your nearest Jobcentre Plus office or you can download a Bereavement Benefits pack from the Department for Work and Pensions website www.dwp.gov.uk or from www.direct.gov.uk

There are many other sites on the web that can help you from widows' support groups to bereavement groups and social networking and dating sites.